D0760836

HUMVEES

BY JACK DAVID

BELLWETHER MEDIA · MINNEAPOLIS, MN

Are you ready to take it to the extreme?
Torque books thrust you into the action-packed
world of sports, vehicles, and adventure. These books
may include dirt, smoke, fire, and dangerous stunts.
WARNING: read at your own risk.

Library of Congress Cataloging-in-Publication Data

David, Jack, 1968-
  Humvees / by Jack David.
      p. cm. – (Torque. Military machines)
  Includes bibliographical references and index.
  Summary: "Amazing photography and engaging information explain the technologies and
capabilities of the Humvee. Intended for students in grades 3 through 7"–Provided by publisher.
  ISBN-13: 978-1-60014-260-4 (hbk. : alk. paper)
  ISBN-10: 1-60014-260-5 (hbk. : alk. paper)
 1. Hummer trucks–Juvenile literature. 2. Military trucks–United States–Juvenile literature. I.
Title.
  UG618.D38 2009
  623.7'4722–dc22   2008035635

This edition first published in 2009 by Bellwether Media, Inc.

No part of this publication may be reproduced in whole or in part without written permission of the
publisher. For information regarding permission, write to Bellwether Media, Inc., Attention:
Permissions Department, Post Office Box 19349, Minneapolis, MN 55419-0349.

Text copyright © 2009 by Bellwether Media, Inc. TORQUE and associated logos are trademarks and/or
registered trademarks of Bellwether Media, Inc.

SCHOLASTIC, CHILDREN'S PRESS, and associated logos are trademarks and/or
registered trademarks of Scholastic Inc.

The photographs in this book are reproduced through the courtesy of the United States Department
of Defense.

Printed in the United States of America.

CONTENTS

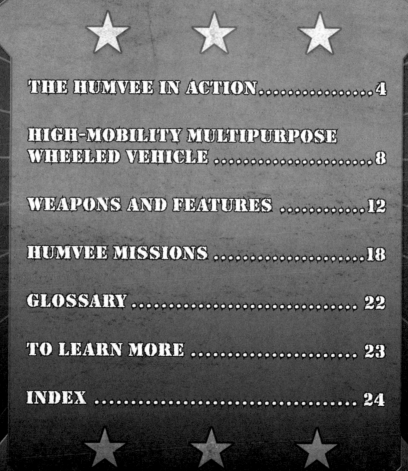

THE HUMVEE IN ACTION

Rocks and dust shoot out from behind the tires of a United States Army Humvee as it rumbles across the desert. The Humvee's crew is on a **mission** to **scout** for signs of enemy activity.

Shots ring out. Enemy fire hits the Humvee, but the bullets bounce off of its strong **armor**. A crew member swings around the Humvee's **machine gun** and returns fire. The gun chatters as it sprays bullets over a wide area. The Humvee driver turns and speeds away to report to base.

HIGH-MOBILITY MULTIPURPOSE WHEELED VEHICLE

Humvee is short for High-Mobility Multipurpose Wheeled Vehicle (HMMWV). The "high-mobility" comes from the Humvee's **four-wheel drive**. The Humvee can use four-wheel drive to travel over any kind of terrain. Its big **diesel** engine can push it to speeds up to 65 miles (105 kilometers) per hour.

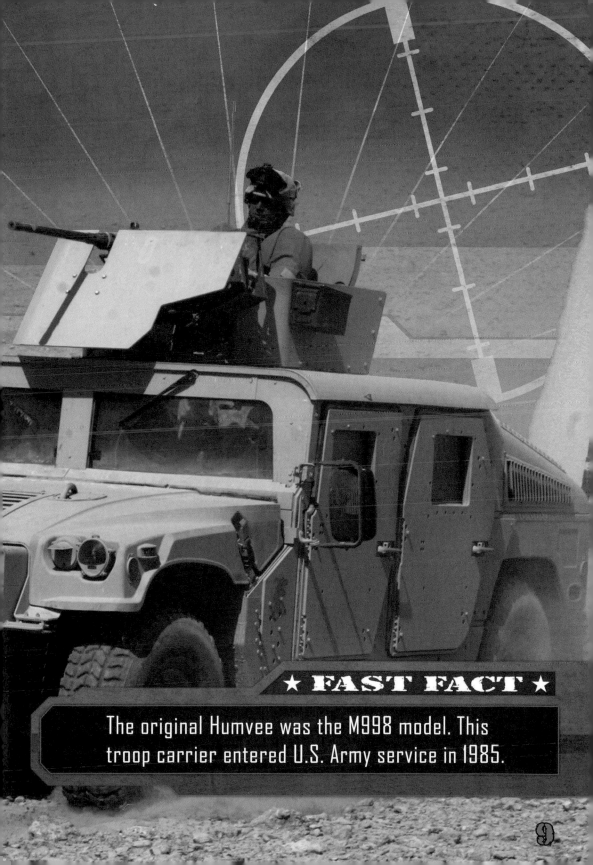

★ **FAST FACT** ★

The original Humvee was the M998 model. This troop carrier entered U.S. Army service in 1985.

The "multipurpose" comes from the many roles a Humvee can take on the battlefield. It can be a troop carrier, a military ambulance, a **missile** carrier, a scout vehicle, and much more. The military can fit it with equipment for all kinds of missions and landscapes.

★ **FAST FACT** ★

Humvees can drive through, or ford, up to 2.5 feet
(.75 meters) of water. With special equipment, they
can go through 5 feet (1.5 meters).

WEAPONS AND FEATURES

A Humvee carries different equipment for different missions. Ambulances carry medical equipment. Some **cargo** and troop carriers are equipped with a **winch** to lift or pull heavy loads.

13

Humvees can also carry a variety of weapons. Many have a gun mounted to the top. These guns, such as the M60 7.62mm machine gun, can turn in any direction. Other Humvees have MK19 **grenade** launchers. Some Humvees pull large missile systems, such as the TOW missile. The TOW is an anti-tank missile that can blast through thick tank armor.

HUMVEE SPECIFICATIONS:

Primary Function: High-mobility multipurpose wheeled vehicle

Length: 15 feet (5 meters)

Width: 7 feet (2 meters)

Height: 6 feet (2 meters)

Weight: 5,200 pounds (2,400 kilograms)

Engine: V8, 6.2-liter diesel

Speed: 65 miles (105 kilometers) per hour

Fuel Capacity: 25 gallons (95 liters)

Range: 350 miles (560 kilometers)

All Humvees have armor. This plating protects the crew from most small arms fire. Certain versions of the Humvee are called "up-armored," because they're equipped with additional armor. These "up-armored" Humvees have armored doors, bullet-resistant windows, and steel plating underneath them to protect them from land mines.

HUMVEE MISSIONS

The Humvee is most often used to transport troops and heavy cargo. Humvees can also rescue injured soldiers on the battlefield, scout out enemy territory, tow large weaponry, and much more.

Different Humvee missions require different crew members. Every Humvee has a driver. Humvees may also have medics and gunners. Medics help injured soldiers. Gunners operate the weaponry.

Humvees have performed many missions since they were first used in the U.S. Army in 1985. Their ability to do many different tasks well has made them valuable to the Army and to the other branches of the **United States Armed Forces**.

GLOSSARY

armor—protective plating made of metal or ceramic materials

cargo—goods carried by a vehicle

diesel—a type of fuel made from oil, commonly used to power large vehicles

four-wheel drive—the ability of a vehicle to provide power to all four of its wheels

grenade—a small explosive that can be thrown or launched with a grenade launcher

machine gun—an automatic weapon that can rapidly fire bullets

missile—an explosive launched at targets on the ground or in the air

mission—a military task

scout—to observe an area using a small force in order to gather information about an enemy

United States Armed Forces—the five branches of the U.S. military; they are the Air Force, the Army, the Coast Guard, the Marine Corps, and the Navy.

winch—a motorized tool that uses strong cables to pull a load

TO LEARN MORE

AT THE LIBRARY

Baker, David. *M1097 Humvee*. Vero Beach, Fla.: Rourke, 2007.

David, Jack. *United States Army*. Minneapolis, Minn.: Bellwether, 2008.

Parker, Steve. *The HMMWV Humvee*. Mankato, Minn.: Capstone, 2008.

ON THE WEB

Learning more about military machines is as easy as 1, 2, 3.

1. Go to www.factsurfer.com.

2. Enter "military machines" into the search box.

3. Click the "Surf" button and you will see a list of related Web sites.

With factsurfer.com, finding more information is just a click away.

INDEX